www.Twelveweeksofgiving.com

Friend us on Facebook:
http://www.facebook.com/pages/12-Weeks-of-Giving/309302259082407

twelve weeks *of* GIVING

AN OFFICE PROJECT IN GIVING

KATHY M. PENNIGAR

Names in this book have been changed to protect individuals' privacy
Scripture taken from the King James Version of the Bible.

The evangelist spoken of in this book is from:
LIFE ACTION MINISTRIES
P.O. Box 31
Buchanan, MI 49107
www.lifeaction.org

WestBow Press books may be ordered through booksellers or by contacting:

WestBow Press
A Division of Thomas Nelson
1663 Liberty Drive
Bloomington, IN 47403
www.westbowpress.com
1-(866) 928-1240

ISBN: 978-1-4497-3019-2 (sc)
ISBN: 978-1-4497-3020-8 (hc)
ISBN: 978-1-4497-3018-5 (e)

Library of Congress Control Number: 2011919848

Printed in the United States of America
WestBow Press rev. date: 11/01/2011

This book is dedicated to my husband of thirty-three years, Josef M. Pennigar. Joe has always believed in me. I love him so very much!

To my children, Jesica and Kristofer, whose childhood passed so fast. I am so honored to be your mother. I love you two very much!

To my children's spouses, Robert, and Jenifer: you have made my children so happy, and I think of you as my very own. I love you very much!

To my grandchildren, Eddie, Robbie, and Peyton, who give me great joy every day: I love you very much.

Introduction

Giving in itself is a gift. If you have been blessed, you should bless someone else. There are many Bible verses on giving, because God expects us to give.

Many therapists say that if you are depressed, you should give to someone else. Look around, and it will not take you long to find someone less fortunate than you. When you give with the love of God, it yields unspeakable joy!

That is what this book is about. Our office staff spent twelve weeks of giving, and the joy was spread throughout two offices and out into the streets. While helping others, we forgot about our problems, which seemed very small anyway.

Joy comes when you give. You may think you have nothing to give; however, giving is not just monetary gifts. Everyone has something to give, such as time, encouragement, and so on.

Hopefully, after reading this book, you will take on a project of your own. It can be individual or a group project. God will bless you beyond belief!

chapter one

Deut. 15:7–8: If there be among you a poor man of one of thy brethren within any of thy gates in thy land which the LORD thy God giveth thee, thou shalt not harden thine heart, nor shut thine hand from thy poor brother: But thou shalt open thine hand wide unto him, and shalt surely lend him sufficient for his need, *in that* which he wanteth.

It was the tenth night of revival led by Life Action Ministries when the idea first came to me. The evangelist was speaking on prayer. The night before, the subject was "Giving." From the screen, I wrote what the evangelist said about *living and giving.* I must be willing to give today out of abundance, to supply the needs of others *believing* that tomorrow, if I have a need, God will use the abundance of others to meet my needs.

Since the revival had started, I had gone to work, sharing with our employees the message that this evangelist had brought to our local church. From the start, I knew there was something special about this revival. I knew that not only was I going to be blessed, but also the company that my husband and I owned. Our employees told us they took the information we gave them home to their loved ones and had a nightly discussion on the subject from the revival the night before.

Back to the ninth night, "Giving," the evangelist said, "Jesus passes by the self-sufficient." I remember when I first learned the *joy* of giving. We were not rich, so the things I gave were modest. Perhaps I would give a poem in calligraphy to someone who was going through a hard time, or a few groceries to someone who was out of work or having trouble. I also remember giving someone groceries, and they told me they gave some of them to another person. I said, "Oh, really?" but was put out, thinking, *I gave this to you because you need it and I did not want you to give it away.* I thought they were ungrateful.

But then God spoke to me: "You know how good it makes you feel to give to someone. Why would you take that joy from them? Not only did you give to someone, but you gave enough so that they could also experience the joy of giving." I felt as though God had spanked me. I was truly ashamed. It is the same principle when you give to the church. It is not for you to worry how the money is spent. One should give in order to be obedient to God. It is all of God's anyway.

When Jesus came to this earth as a baby, He did not come as a wealthy person. There is no one wealthier than He, but He did not choose to be prideful. Not only is Christ wealthier than everyone, He is also more intelligent than all of us. There are so many things that we are unable to comprehend because we do not have the wisdom He has.

The evangelist asked on this ninth night that we give tomorrow in abundance, to supply the needs of someone. He asked us to pray about it so that God would put someone in our path. Later, one of our former employees we had not seen in years came in to talk with me.

She was beautiful, inside and out. She had the love of God in her, as evidenced by her compassion for others. She said, "I have been on disability for a few years due to an auto accident. I broke my legs, my pelvis, and an ankle. My doctor wants me to try and find a job that is not too strenuous, since my bones are still healing and I become easily fatigued." She also stated, "I have been broken, inside and out, and I am here today to talk to you and to try my best not to cry, since I know this is how God wants me to be."

I totally forgot about giving in abundance or giving at all, however, I just felt that God was telling me to write her a check. My husband and I agreed that $200 seemed like a good amount. I took the check to her and said, "I do not have a sitting job as you described or a client that only needs to be monitored, but I have this check for you, and I will do some research with other companies and see if I can find you an office job or something."

My dear sister in Christ wept. "I did not come here for money, but thank you," she said.

I said, "I know you didn't, but God has blessed us, and you would help me if I needed it."

This was the perfect time for me to share revival with her. I told her that the evangelist from Life Action Ministries told us that God doesn't fault anyone for having savings accounts or retirement plans unless those things become our security. God wants us to depend on Him. Many people who have riches think they do not need God, since they are self-sufficient. It is easy to have faith when you have thousands of dollars in a bank account, but can you have the same faith if you live from paycheck to paycheck?

God has brought me through fifty-one years without starving, and we have had a roof over our heads, so I think He will do the same in the future. If it is not the same roof in the future, I have to believe that God knows much more than I know. I have peace, which comes from God.

On the tenth night, I was sitting in a pew, listening to people give their testimonies on the wonderful things that God has done for them the past ten nights. Many of them talked about forgiveness and pride, and how God had taken away their pride, enabling them to ask their friends', co-workers', or loved ones' forgiveness. One lady said that she was giving her dad the time that she had been taking from him.

"Giving"; there's that word again, and then I felt God speaking to me. I felt He was telling me to make a teaching experience out of giving for all of our office employees. This would be a lesson for all of us.

We have two women whose husbands lost their jobs. The economy spiraled down the past few years, causing one of them to lose his, while another lost his job to disability. His health had deteriorated, and he could no longer drive, since he was passing out and his doctor told him that he could no longer work.

I came home very excited. My husband and son did not go this particular night, because both of them were taking college Bible classes. When I shared this plan that God had laid on my heart, my husband told me that we needed some guidelines. We have nine people in the office. My idea was that each week we give $100 to one person. We ask that person to take the money and share as many blessings as possible. When he or she has spent the last cent, then he or she will come back and report to everyone, so that we can all enjoy the blessings.

My idea was that by the time we got to the ninth person, the blessings would be increased, since each person would be motivated by the person before him, and their sphere of influence would be different. This money would be stretched as far as a group of people could possibly stretch it; I felt sure each person would get ideas from various sources.

My husband, Joe, and I were very excited to get the "giving project" started. This was going to be a blessing and a learning experience for all of us! Joe suggested we draw the first recipient's name the next day. I could hardly sleep; I was so excited. This was also a praying lesson, so that we could all pray for each other. This was not a competition but a project that would involve all of our office staff.

In the Bible, Luke 6:38 (KJV), Jesus said, "Give, and it shall be given unto you; good measure, pressed down, and shaken together, and running over, shall men give unto your bosom. For with the same measure that ye mete withal it shall be measured to you again."

This project reminded me of the talents given to three men in Matthew 25:15–30. One man was given five talents, another two, and another one. The man with five talents traded with the same and made them five other talents. He that had two also gained two. The man who was given one talent hid the talent in the earth. Their lord was happy with the first two men, but to the one who hid his in the earth told him in Matthew 25:27, "Thou oughtest therefore to have put my money to the exchangers, and then at my coming I should have received mine own with usury." Then in Matthew 25:29, "For unto every one that hath shall be given, and he shall have abundance: but from him that hath not shall be taken away even that which he hath."

chapter two

Deut. 16:17 Every man *shall give* as he is able, according to the blessing of the LORD thy God which he hath given thee.

When we arrived at work, we called everyone into the conference room and told them what we were doing. Our oldest employee, whom everyone trusts, drew the name. It was Jenifer.

We talked about different ways to help people and urged them to come up with even more ideas. Several of our employees gave ideas, and all agreed to pray for the one whose name was drawn for the week. One employee offered, "If you are talking about stretching the money, I could go have two thousand copies made of Bible verses and put on windshields at shopping centers, and I would have stretched the money farther."

I said, "You are right, and that is why we are praying that God will help that person to make the right decision."

Everyone was excited, which made me even more excited. Then, as we were sitting there, in walked someone needing a drug screening for employment. The two companies that my husband and I own (or actually run, since they both belong to God) are Jeskri Associates, Inc., an employment drug screening company, and Neighborhood Nurses Health Care Services, Inc., a nursing agency. We send nurses or certified nursing assistants into the homes of patients who are sick or terminal.

Jenifer is our office manager, and she is also a certified nursing assistant. She started with Neighborhood Nurses when we first opened in 2002. She is twenty-five years old and married to my son Kris. She is very beautiful, and she and Kris have given us our first granddaughter,

Peyton, who has the most beautiful eyes I've ever seen. Everyone comments on Peyton's eyes, no matter where we go. She has blue eyes like both of her Nanas. However, one of her Nanas is deceased.

Jenifer's mom passed away at the young age of forty-two, when Jenifer was pregnant with Peyton. She was an alcoholic, and though she was a very compassionate person, it wasn't enough to save her from the grip that alcohol had on her. My father was also gripped by alcohol, and that makes for a difficult life for everyone. My son chose Jenifer for his bride, and I could not have chosen a better fit for our family had I been the one to choose.

Jenifer seems like a daughter to me. We understand each other very well. We have so much in common. Sometimes my son accuses me—jokingly, of course—of loving her more than I love him.

The gentleman who came in for the drug screen told the drug tech that he didn't know how he was going to get the results back to his employer, since he had no gasoline for his car. Tommy slipped away and told everyone that he wished he was chosen this week, so he could help the gentleman. Immediately, everyone who had extra cash jumped up, got the cash, and discretely took it in to the gentleman. I saw his face. He was overwhelmed, and I believe he didn't know what to say. He thanked everyone and then left. We were all excited that we knew he could drive and have a nice meal.

Already there was something special taking place, which got everyone even more excited about the "giving" project. Jenifer was to give us a full report of her week next Wednesday. Meanwhile, we would all be praying that God would give her guidance.

Jenifer left for lunch and came back smiling. I said, "Why are you smiling?"

She asked, "Do I have to wait until next Wednesday to tell what I did with part of the money?"

I said, "Yes." Then I said, "But you can tell me."

She had called the Crisis Pregnancy Center and asked them what their needs were. She then went and bought bottles, diapers, shampoo, blankets, pacifiers, and trash bags and delivered them to the center. This took $40 of her money. Her smile was worth $1,000!

Joe and I have always known that Neighborhood Nurses is our ministry. So we have tried to help people who we know are in need. Every Christmas, we ask our Sunday school classes in our church to help fill stockings for our patients. We have pediatrics to geriatrics, and they have always enjoyed getting the stockings every year. In fact, if they do not get them in a reasonable amount of time, they call asking for them. The stockings are a perfect opportunity to witness to people while showing the love of God. I am always amazed at the unique items that people put in the stockings—things I never would have thought of but things that people really enjoy. We put fruit, candy, and nuts in them to spark their memory of years ago, when that is all many people could afford at Christmas.

Jenifer has always had a giving spirit. She was raised by her daddy and paternal grandparents. I remember her grandmother dying while Jenifer was in high school. It broke my heart, because this woman was like a mother to her. Jenifer was a timid young lady and had very few words to say, but you could see the pain in her eyes. Jenifer had a complex life that I'm sure would take up the space of a book alone. That is her story to tell. I just want everyone to get an idea of the wonderful person she is.

When Peyton was born, she allowed me along with my son to be in the birth room. Since I am an RN, I was able to help. Nothing is as special to me as seeing the birth of a grandchild. I was also fortunate enough to be present when my daughter, Jesica, had her first son. I could not stop crying. I was embarrassed because I could not control my tears. The tears were happy tears, of course. This was our first grandchild.

On the tenth night of revival, the evangelist touched on giving again. I wanted to shout out, "We've got what you have been teaching, and we are giving." Giving is not just about monetary gifts. One can give time to many things such as reading God's Word and doing things for others. Sometimes giving of our time is more valuable than giving money. Just as we told our employees, after the completion of the $100 giving, we also wanted to draw names and have them give one of their days to helping others. They would be on our payroll clock as they did this. All of them agreed that this would be another good project. Many of our clients have needs.

We have a satellite office in Wadesboro. Our son, Kristofer (Kris) manages the Wadesboro Neighborhood Nurses and the Wadesboro Jeskri Associates. He came by as we were doing the drawing and requested that we do the same for his office. There are three people who work in the office there, bringing our office staff to a total of twelve people. Now the "giving project" has already grown. I was so impressed that he also wanted the three of them to join in.

Peyton & Jenifer
(Kathy's daughter in law, Kristofer's wife)

Kathy's son, Kristofer & his daughter, Peyton

Kathy's oldest grandson, Eddie (Jesica's son)

Jesica (Kathy's daughter)

Robbie (Kathy's youngest grandson)
(Jesica's son)

chapter three

Mark 12:41–44 And Jesus sat over against the treasury, and beheld how the people cast money into the treasury: and many that were rich cast in much. And there came a certain poor widow, and she threw in two mites, which make a farthing. And he called *unto him* his disciples, and saith unto them, Verily I say unto you, That this poor widow hath cast more in, than all they which have cast into the treasury: For all *they* did cast in of their abundance; but she of her want did cast in all that she had, *even* all her living.

During those days, the Lord spoke to me and reminded me of a time when I was a child. Many times when we had Bible school and even regular church services, my mom was unable to attend for one reason or another. We had one set of neighbors who always went to church and always passed by our house. My mom would instruct my younger brother and me to stand beside the mailbox, and surely they would pick us up so we could go.

When the Lord laid this on my heart, I thought, *Well, they were going right by our house, so it wasn't like they were going out of their way,* and I felt Him saying, "But they were responsible for two more children." And a light came on inside my head. I sent a basket of goodies to their home, thanking them for taking us to church and telling them that I had good memories of going with them. God also reminded me of the many times they took us to the swimming pool while our mom was working.

I am not telling the story about the neighbors to ring my bell. I am hoping someone who reads this will remember a similar deed and go back and thank someone too. If you do not have monetary gifts to give, encouragement would be a nice gift to give.

That incident sparked another childhood memory. One of those times that our neighbor had taken us to church, I was using the bathroom, and a little girl came running by me and fell. I was eleven years old, and my first instinct was to ignore her and let an adult take care of her. I did, however, go over to her and wiped the small blue rocks from her knee. I then asked her if she was okay. After she stopped crying and I knew she was okay, I went on my way.

A couple of weeks later, the little girl's mom came to my house and told my mom what had happened. I had no idea that this little girl would remember and certainly didn't believe she could tell her mom about the incident or tell her that it was me who helped her. Her mom went on to tell my mom that because of my maturity, she would like me to babysit both of her daughters. Wow! I had a job at eleven years old. I enjoyed my job.

My mom told me, "Always do more than what is expected of you, and you will always have a job."

I said, "What do you mean?"

She said, "If she asks you to feed the girls, then wash the dishes and sweep the floor."

I remember taking care of them and washing the dishes, just as my mom had suggested. I also remember them jumping on the bed and me joining them. So I wasn't *that* mature. I always had fun with them, though. Many benefits came with the job. The family took me places with them, including parades and fairs, and they paid me too.

I believe all good deeds are rewarded in one way or another. This reminds me of what the evangelist said on the tenth night: "Until God can trust you on the little things, He will not put you in charge of bigger things." The evangelist said that when he went into a public restroom, he used to wash his hands and practice his long shot on the trash can. He said that when he missed the can, he did not pick it up, since he knew someone would be cleaning the bathroom and they could pick it up. But then God convicted him, and he had to pick it up. Now he admits that he always places his used towels in the trash can.

When you think no one is watching, just remember God is, and He is the one that truly counts. God is the one we need to please.

The second day after Jenifer's name was drawn, she went to a Christian bookstore and bought bibles. She said that she had thought about it and prayed about it and felt led to purchase bibles to put on people's windshields. She said that she was working on a note that she wanted to put with the bibles. Jenifer is very creative and very computer literate. She set up the most fascinating website for those who received the bibles. She put the website address on the note so that they could go to the website and request prayers, make comments, and most of all she told them how to receive Jesus into their lives. I was very proud of her! She had such wonderful ideas. Again, I got so excited just knowing we had eleven more weeks of giving to go.

On the last night of revival, the evangelist informed us that God did not make us for our pleasure. He made us for *His* pleasure. He made each person with a purpose for their life. It is our responsibility to find our purpose. We learn this through reading God's Word, praying, and getting close to Him. There's no one happier than the person who is in God's will. The world cannot offer you peace, love, or anything that God can give you.

As I said before, it doesn't cost anything to give the gift of encouragement. I had the opportunity to give a young lady words of encouragement. She was having a difficult time because her mom had died two years ago and her daddy remarried. She was close to her mom and hurt that her dad's attention was totally on his new family. I told her that her life would not always be sad. I told her to pray and ask God to send her the gentleman He created for her. That is what I did at a very young age, and He sent me my soul mate!

This young lady told me that the guys she had dated were definitely not who she thought God would want her with and that she was going to pray for the right one. She said she would love to have someone really care about her, because she did not feel like her daddy did, and her heart was broken for her mom.

Encouragement is free. Perhaps God gave you a gift to encourage others. People need to be encouraged. We should pray that He will give us people to encourage. When someone is going through a difficult time, they want to hear from someone who has been there.

chapter four

Ps. 112:9 He hath dispersed, he hath given to the poor; his righteousness endureth for ever; his horn shall be exalted with honour.

In October of 1995, my mother was diagnosed with breast cancer. The tumor was four and a half centimeters in size and had spread to her lymph nodes. The oncologist told me that he didn't think she was a candidate for chemotherapy, and he didn't think she would make the five-year mark. My heart was broken. I remember my husband and I were out driving and we came upon a pumpkin patch. I wanted to get out of the car and burst every pumpkin I could get my hands on.

At times, I was inconsolable. I only wanted to hear from people who had been there. I remember working third shift with a patient in their home, a pediatric child. When the parents went to bed, I cried all night. I prayed and pleaded with God. I told Him, "God, I cannot do without my mother now."

Her primary doctor did not like that the oncologist seemed to give up on her and referred her to another one. The new one thought her life was worth trying to save and ordered chemotherapy.

My dad's health was bad, so I took my mom back and forth to the doctor and to chemotherapy after her mastectomy. My two brothers helped as much as they could. My older brother, Randy, with his tender heart, came up to me one day and said, "Sis, I'm not as strong as you and Tommy; I can't be around Mama without crying, so if you take her to chemotherapy, I will give you anything she needs or pay for it." He was sobbing as he was speaking to me. He said, "I just hope and pray that I die before any of my family, because I couldn't take burying any of you."

My mom's hair fell out while she was at the beauty shop. My teenage daughter was with her. She came and woke me up when my mom brought her home. I had worked third shift, and Jesica came into my bedroom and said, "Mom, you have got to get up. Grandma is crying because her hair fell out."

This hurt me very much. Throughout my childhood, it seems, I spent much of my life in a beauty salon with my mom. She went weekly to have her hair styled. She actually seemed obsessed with her hair. It was definitely her glory. The pain I experienced seeing her cry was almost unbearable. I just held on to her.

Fortunately, a few weeks before, we had gone to a boutique, where she tried wigs on my head. She did not want to mess her hair up, so she had the lady put them on me. We got a lot of laughs at the time, but she still had her hair.

I watched as my mom went through different stages of grief. During her anger stage, we ate salads after chemotherapy. This was because she was told not to eat them. Mom and I always stopped by Marshall's before her chemotherapy. The initial day that we went for her diagnostic mammogram we stopped in Marshall's. She and I went different ways in the store and I thought I heard her calling me. The voice was sad. I said, "Yeah, Mama" and turned and there was no one there. This happened about three times. Then I knew she had breast cancer. I thought that God must be getting me ready so that I could be strong for her.

Sure enough, I was called back and shown the X-rays. The radiologist explained everything to me. I was strong for my mom, but as soon as I got her home and made my own way home, the tears flowed. Standing in a grocery store, tears flowed from me. Then I realized, there must be others who are walking around as hurt as I am, and I hoped people were kind to them, since I knew I could not take any more hurt of any kind.

Mom and I were in an auto accident one day when we stopped to shop. Someone just rammed into us. It was an accident, though. We didn't get hurt, but my car did. My mom and I became even closer during this time.

We had about a year's worth of very bad happenings from 1995 to 1996. My daughter got her driver's license and totaled her car, almost killing another person. My children's pediatrician—whom I trusted with my child who had apnea and seizures and my precious daughter too—died from post-polio syndrome. I cried like a baby. This wonderful pediatrician had treated me many times. Several times I took my children to him when I was also sick. He saved me time and money that I would have spent going to another doctor. Most times, he waived my co-payment and said, "I need some calligraphy, so let's just trade." I doubt he needed as much calligraphy as he had me do.

My mom finished her chemotherapy and seemed to be getting along great. She was still wearing wigs, because her hair had not yet grown out. As soon as I knew she was stable, my husband, children, and I went to the Poconos, to a camp where we had worked for the past four years. I worked in the infirmary, and my husband was a transportation director. We wanted our children to attend, but because I am very protective, I wanted to be with them. Besides, we could not have afforded it had we not worked there. This time we only stayed two weeks instead of the whole summer.

We came back late Saturday. I had scheduled myself to work that Sunday night. I didn't go to see my family that Sunday, because I had so much to do to get unpacked and be ready to work a twelve-hour shift on Sunday, 7:00 p.m. to 7:00 a.m. My plan was to visit them on Monday.

I came home from work around 7:30 a.m. My normal routine was to put my pajamas on and go straight to bed when I came home, after I had hugged my children and husband and told them I loved them. Something was different about this morning. Strangely, I put on shorts, got the phone, and placed it on the floor beside the sofa where I decided to sleep. I do not know why I did that. I wasn't expecting a phone call, and no one was sick that I knew of.

After I had slept a couple of hours, the telephone rang. I picked it up, and it was my older brother, Randy. He said, "Sis, I am dying."

"What?" I said.

He said, "My chest is hurting, and I am dying."

In nursing school, we were taught that when someone tells you they are dying to believe them, since they usually know. But this was my big brother. I said, "No, Randy, you are not dying." I couldn't think straight. I said, "Randy, I'm calling 911," and he said no. I said, "They have drugs on the truck that will take away your pain," and he agreed. I hung the phone up, called EMS, and said, "I am a nurse; my brother is having a heart attack and I cannot get to him fast enough, so please go help him."

I then called Randy, who never picked up the phone. I got his answering machine and told him to go and open the door because they were on their way.

I drove eighty miles an hour to his house while I was still in a daze. When I got there, the ambulance was leaving with him. I called around and found my parents, picked them up, and sped to the hospital. When I got to the ER, he was hooked up to a heart monitor. After observing his vitals and seeing him in excruciating pain, I knew this did not look good.

Three years earlier, he had a heart attack while playing softball. He was thirty-six years old. When we got to the hospital, we were told he had a 50 percent chance of living, because he was in cardiogenic shock. My mom and I got down on a dirty bathroom floor and pleaded with God for his life. God saved him. He had not had any further problems since then, so this was a total shock.

This time I knew God was taking him home. I knew in my heart that this was the day, and there was no need to plead his case on my knees. When the doctor decided to put a pacemaker in before flying him to another hospital, I begged the cardiologist to let me go in with him so I could stay with my brother. He said, "If this was my brother, I would want someone to keep me from going back with him."

I said, "But I won't cry or get in your way." All the while, tears were gushing down my face.

Many of my nurse friends sat with me in the family waiting room. Instead of calling a code, because they knew I was a nurse, they just called, "Respiratory to the cath lab."

I said, "He has died." All of my friends tried to convince me it was not necessarily so, but I knew he was gone. My heart was crushed. He was dead, leaving two small children, a wife, and us.

Later, the hardest thing was looking over at my mom, standing beside his casket, wearing her wig on family night. I was drugged like a zombie. My doctor medicated me the maximum dose he could without putting me to sleep. I was very close to my brother. Being in a zombie state still did not hide the pain of watching my parents bury their thirty-nine-year-old son. He died on my husband's birthday.

Madge and Roy (Kathy's parents)

BROTHER

Your life's memory
Is like a trinket that
I wear.

Reminding me daily
Of the existence that
We had.

Reminiscence is opening
The trinket, feeling
Your spirit, and
Hearing your laughter.

You exited life early,
Before I could tell
You what you
Really meant
To me.

If I could go back,
I would drop the
Sibling arrogance
And confess you
Were **ASTOUNDING!**

Kathy Mullis Pennigar

Randy (Kathy's older brother)
09-09–1957-08–26–1996

chapter five

Mal. 3:10 Bring ye all the tithes into the storehouse, that there may be meat in mine house, and prove me now herewith, saith the LORD of hosts, if I will not open you the windows of heaven, and pour you out a blessing, that *there shall* not *be room* enough *to receive it.*

During the week that Jenifer was doing her good deeds with the money that was given to her, several of our employees were sitting in the kitchen having a break. One of our employees said, "I have a problem."

I said, "And that is?"

"I do not know how to go about this when my name is drawn."

I asked, "What do you mean?"

"I don't know what to say to someone."

Another of our employees said, "If I were poor or needed something, I wouldn't care what you said. I would just be thankful that someone gave me something."

I had to tell her about an opportunity that my husband and I had to give that morning. We stopped by a fast-food restaurant to get some unsweetened tea. While there, a lady came up pushing a shopping cart containing an overnight bag bursting at the seams with all sorts of things. I told my husband that I wished I had some cash with me to give her. He had four dollars in his pocket. I said that was not enough. He replied, "If she is hungry, it will buy her a biscuit and drink." We drove around, and there were several people around her, waiting to order and making fun of her for the shopping cart she was pushing.

I told my husband that he should call her over to the side so that he would not embarrass her. He gave her the money, and she was shocked. She said, "I can't take this."

He said, "I would like to buy your breakfast this morning."

She held the money up and looked puzzled. The people around her looked even more puzzled. We told her to have a good day and went on our way.

I was confused when we left since I didn't understand why she looked so surprised. It's not every day you go to a restaurant and see someone pushing a shopping cart. I am aware that God likes us to give in secret, and when we tell, we are getting the reward at that time. But this is a project in giving; therefore, I feel I should share our experiences. All experiences in giving may not feel so comfortable to you, but when you feel God wants you to give, then you should give. You may not know God's entire plan, but He does, and we should just be obedient.

My mom and I were shopping one Saturday and stopped at a restaurant to have lunch. The waitress was a pretty young lady with a very sweet personality. She had a lot of tables and seemed to be doing a great job keeping everyone happy. I could not see the lady sitting in the booth behind me, but when the waitress brought out her food, she became very nasty!

The customer said, "Oh, no, this is not how I like my steak. I like it medium rare."

The waitress said, "It is supposed to be medium rare,"

The customer then said, "Oh, how do you know? You never asked me how I wanted my steak cooked." The customer went on and on. The waitress was trying very hard to be accommodating while offering to have another steak cooked for her. "No," she said.

Pretty soon the waitress's whole countenance had changed. I felt very sorry for her. Nothing she did pleased the customer. The customer ended up asking to talk to the manager and bashed the waitress really badly.

Meanwhile, the waitress, all anxious, brought my bill to me. I wrote a note on my ticket stating that the lady sitting behind me was a complainer and that it is her personality. Then I started with my personal giving project and gave her three dollars extra after I gave the tip.

When I got home, I discussed this with my husband. We decided that both of us should be giving simultaneously while our employees are giving, so that the project will be completed two weeks earlier.

The next day, we took our son and his family out to eat for his birthday. When we arrived at the restaurant, I started joking with the waiter. Three members of our party were in the bathroom, and he thought that was funny. He then said it seemed good to have some happy customers. I asked, "You mean people come in here in bad moods?"

He said, "Lately, everyone that has come in have brought their problems and take them out on me. People are just so rude."

He was a very good waiter, being mindful of our needs. I told him that it was my son's birthday and asked if they would sing to him. He told me that recently a family came in and asked them to sing to their daughter. The daughter later reported them to the corporate office and was very irate in doing so, and now they were not allowed to sing to customers. He said, "One person ruined it for everyone. I am thirty-four years old and have to work, but I do not understand why people are so hostile."

When he brought the ticket, my husband gave him a generous tip, but I was led to give him a five-dollar bill, just to let him know he was appreciated. I am aware that three or five dollars is not a lot of money, but remember, I only have a hundred dollars with which to do my good deeds in this project.

Jenifer finished her giving for the week and was very excited to tell everyone how she spent the money. Everyone was seated around the table as she discussed her blessings. The receivers were not the only ones blessed. It was evident that Jenifer received a huge blessing in giving. Her eyes lit up, as did the smile on her face, as she told them that she called the Crisis Pregnancy Center to see what their needs were.

Everyone was impressed to know that she had a passion for young ladies who had decided to keep their babies instead of aborting them, regardless of the situations. The ten bibles that Jenifer purchased from the Christian bookstore were wrapped with a Bible verse neatly tucked into each one, along with a note telling them how to accept Jesus Christ into their lives. This gift should keep on giving, after she set up the website.

The remaining money, $37, Jenifer gave to one of her husband's best friends they both went to school with. They found out that his wife of seven years left him and their four children. Jenifer not only gave the $37 that she had left over, but took up more money from our office employees, since he was coming to the office. After cleaning our purses, cars, and change from all of the drawers, we came up with a total of $89. Then Joe decided that he wanted to give all of his hundred dollars to this friend. I was impressed; I knew Joe had been tossing other ideas around in his head about his giving.

The friend was overwhelmed that we would care that much about him to help him. We told him that we would help with his children's Christmas instead of choosing names that we do not know from the angel tree. We also offered him free babysitting services and anything else he had a need for. He programmed our phone numbers into his phone and assured us that he would call us.

chapter six

Prov. 22:9 He that hath a bountiful eye shall be blessed; for he giveth of his bread to the poor.

When Wednesday came around, we drew Linda's name from our Wadesboro office. Kris took the money to her. Linda had thought about the project and had decided that she would purchase ducks for Paraguay, so the poor people there could raise them, sell the eggs, and have ducks to eat. She had thought long and hard about this and how she could get the most out of the money. When she heard about Kris's friend, she went into his office and said, "I had planned to purchase the ducks, however, I believe we need to take care of our people here at home first, so would you please give the money to your friend so that he and his children can benefit."

Kris was touched that she would give to his friend whom she had never met. Kris was not shocked, though. He had always respected Linda and choices that she made. The two of them had always gotten along very well.

Linda is around sixty but looks much younger. She is a beautiful lady in looks and personality. She has been very beneficial to our company, because she knows just about everyone in the area. Linda and her husband are always there to help others in need. They have one daughter, who is beautiful like her mom.

Kris really got into the giving and once again went around the office to see if he could get even more money to give to his friend. Along with the $100, he collected $30 more to go with it. He called his friend to come to the office.

Meanwhile, Jenifer and I decided that we would start on the Christmas gifts for the children. We purchased each one an outfit, pajamas, a toy laptop that was age-appropriate, and another toy. We checked with the grandmother to make sure these were items that could be used. She told us that she would also help with Christmas.

Matthew 6:2–4 says, "When you give to the needy, do not announce it with trumpets, as the hypocrites do in the synagogues and on the streets, to be honored by men. I tell you the truth; they have received their reward in full. But when you give to the needy, do not let your left hand know what your right hand is doing, so that your giving may be in secret. Then your Father, who sees what is done in secret, will reward you."

According to those verses, everything that we are doing will not be rewarded, since we are publishing in this book. This book is not written as a "trumpet-sounding" book; I just want people to learn to give. There is no better feeling than that of helping someone. No one expects it, as evidenced by the shocking expressions that we have seen.

Rhonda works in our Monroe office. She does our billing, drug screens, and a lot of other important tasks around the office. She is in her forties and married with two furry children (puppy dogs). She worked at a university for twenty-five years prior to coming to work with Neighborhood Nurses. When the next Wednesday came around, Rhonda's name was pulled.

Last year, Rhonda's husband's health declined, and he was forced to file for disability. The process took a year, and they lived without any income from him. This was very difficult on both of them, because he also lost his driving privileges due to a medical condition that caused him to pass out.

When the head of the household loses their job, regardless of the reason, it makes it difficult on the family. I am sure Rhonda could write a whole book on the ups and downs that they went through and how their family dynamics changed.

My husband lost his job in 1992, and it was very difficult for him. Joe has given me permission to tell his story, to help others who have lost jobs. Many people lose their jobs when the economy gets bad and many businesses close.

When my husband left his job to go to work for one of his former employer's competitors, who had been my husband's friend for many years, he knew he could never go back to the position he was leaving. One of my friends reminded me that the company that he was going to work for had a reputation of laying people off. I thought, he won't lay my husband off, since they are good friends. He wasn't there a year and this company let him go.

My husband felt used, since this company learned everything that he knew and then let him go. He had many years in the industry in which he was trained, but he had been unable to find another job because computers had taken over a lot of the industry.

Every day, I could see my husband becoming more and more depressed. I've heard it said that the eyes are the windows to one's soul, and it was his eyes that scared me so. They looked so empty. I gladly picked up extra hours. After all, my husband worked overtime in 1987 so that I could fulfill my dream of becoming a nurse. He ironed my uniforms when I had to be at a hospital for clinicals and had to leave at 4:00 a.m. He worked as hard for my nursing license as I did.

During this time when he seemed so depressed, I heard about a camp in the Poconos of Pennsylvania where nurses could go to work while their children attended the camp for free. Also, the spouses were given jobs according to their talents. This was awesome, because my husband could work on automobiles and do anything else a handyman could do.

I talked him into it and got the okay from the two jobs that I worked to be off for a whole summer and then resume my positions when we returned.

The summer experience at the camp was wonderful. My husband, Joe, was having a fantastic time. The owners took to him right away, and he became their right-hand man. He picked children up from the airport, fixed everything that broke, and still had time to spend with our family, since we got a couple of days off weekly. We saw the Statue of Liberty for the first time, as well as many other places in New York, New Jersey, and Pennsylvania.

One day, he was driving some campers back to the airport, and the van broke down. He got under it to fix it, and gasoline poured onto his face. When he came back to camp, he was feeling really bad. He actually passed out while we were watching one of our children's plays.

That night, his temperature spiked to 105, and he started coughing violently. He was hospitalized for several weeks. I was a basket case. I wondered how I would get him home or *if* I would get him home.

The hospital was very small. I asked his doctor if we could move him to a larger hospital in New York, and he said Joe was not stable enough. Every day when I went to the hospital, the doctor told me that he didn't really know how to treat Joe, because everyone he knew who ingested gasoline usually died. I was devastated!

Joe lost about fifty pounds, and I was losing weight too, because I would not eat. I prayed and pleaded with God to heal my husband. One day, one of the other nurses who worked in ICU in Florida called her large hospital and talked to the pulmonologist there, who said the doctor in the small hospital should wash Joe's lungs. The two doctors talked, and the one at the small hospital did the procedure.

When I came back to the hospital, the doctor told me again that it almost looked like a pneumonitis, because the inflammation was spreading. I went into my husband's room and started pleading with him to get well. I cried and told him that I didn't even know the way home, because I was not paying attention and there was no such thing as GPS then. I said, "You could get better if you wanted to!"

My husband said that when he saw how big a baby I was, he knew he had to get well. He said he had always thought that I was so independent and could do anything without him, but after that, he knew he had to get well.

We brought him home, and the doctors in Charlotte took care of him for several months before he fully recovered. This was my miracle! God heard my prayer. My husband helped me to put the pieces of the puzzle together when we returned home. He told me that he was very depressed before we went to camp. When we got to camp, he said he was very happy because everyone loved his work and made him feel special. He said he knew that when he got home, it would be the same old thing again: depression from not having a job. He said that he had thought about taking his life, because he knew the children and I would benefit more from the life insurance than from him being unemployed. My heart sank.

Then he said, "But I knew I couldn't take my life, because you are a big baby and could not survive without me." I was so glad I showed myself while he was in the hospital that day! God knows things that we do not. Hospitalizing my husband saved his life in more ways than one.

MY HUSBAND/MY FRIEND

My best friend and my husband
Are one and the same,
I get so very happy
At the mention of his name.

A sprightly personality
Occupies my friend,
Courageous, chivalrous nature
To which there is no end.

How lustrous is this man of mine
Who bears to me his soul,
And my sensational vision is that
"TOGETHER WE'LL GROW OLD!"

KATHY MULLIS PENNIGAR

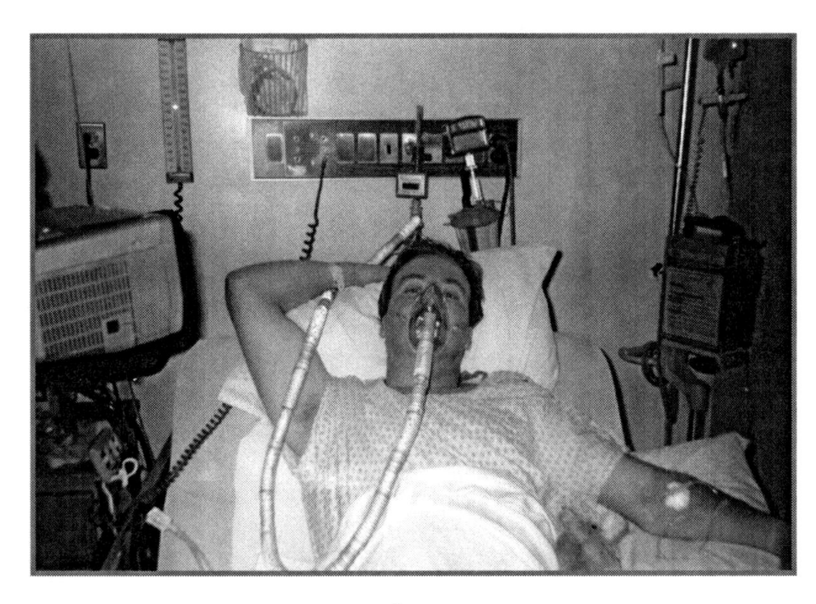

JOE

JOE, KATHY AND JESICA
(CAMP IN THE POCONO MTNS.)

JOSEF (JOE)

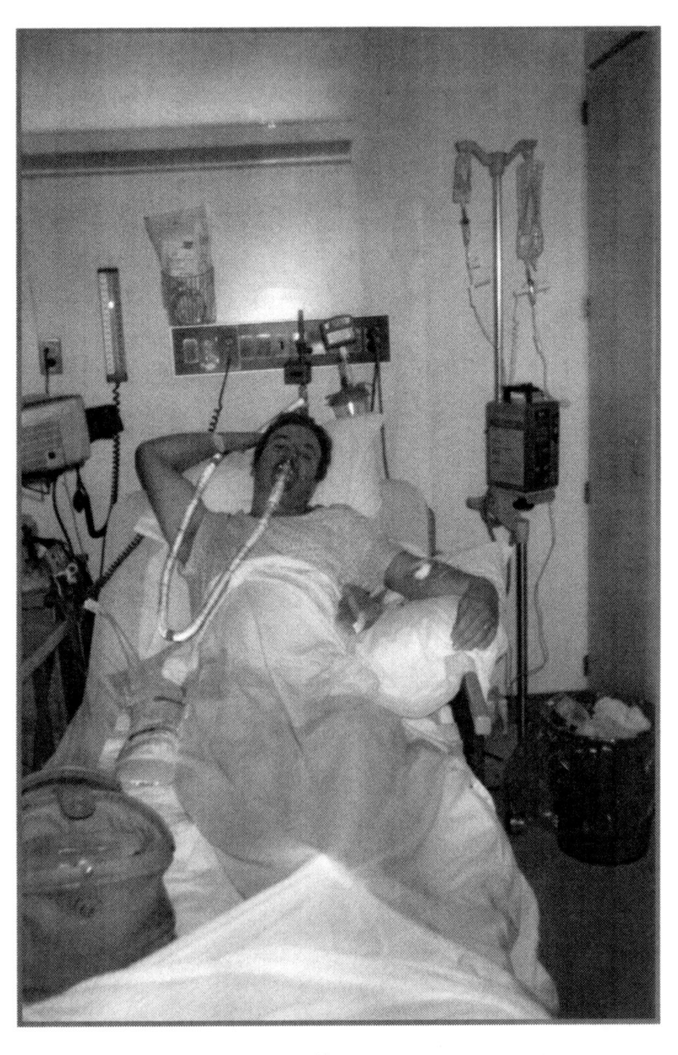

Joe
(Hospital in PA)

chapter seven

Prov. 28:27 He that giveth unto the poor shall not lack: but he that hideth his eyes shall have many a curse.

Proverbs 11:24–25 says, "One man gives freely, yet grows all the richer; another withholds what he should give, and only suffers want. A liberal man will be enriched, and one who waters will himself be watered."

There are so many Bible verses on giving. That lets us know that God intends for us to give. We were so excited to see what Rhonda did with the money. Immediately, Rhonda went to the homeless shelter and asked them how many people were housed there. They told her five women and fourteen men.

Rhonda went to the dollar store and purchased hats, gloves, socks, pantyhose, shampoo, body wash, tissues, candy, lip gloss, and costume jewelry. She also purchased gallon bags and organized the items in the bags. Then she typed John 3:16–17 "For God so loved the world that he gave his only begotten son, that whosoever believeth in him should not perish, but have everlasting life. For God sent his son into the world not to condemn the world; but that the world through him might be saved." She placed the verses on each package.

What a brilliant idea! That was the excitement in seeing the different ideas that each person had. Joe and I could never spread the giving of $1,200 the way the other ten people were doing!

Rhonda was hungry after shopping for the nineteen homeless people at the shelter and decided to drive through a fast-food restaurant and get dinner. She then told the cashier that she wanted to pay for the meal for the car behind her. She was on a roll! The lady said, "You want to do what?" Rhonda thought it was funny that she couldn't believe she wanted to pay for their food. Their ticket was $12.05. Rhonda stretched her money, as she had $23 left to spend.

Joe and I stopped that morning at a Subway that is connected to a gas station. I sat in the car while he went in to get our sandwiches. A gentleman drove up in a beat-up truck with a beat-up lawn mower on the back of the truck. His gasoline can was a used antifreeze container. I watched as he pulled out his money from his pocket. It looked as though he had only a couple dollars.

This man put gasoline into his lawn mower. It only took a couple of seconds, so he could not have put in more than a dollar or two, and the same amount for the container. I felt God telling me to give him the $20 that was in my purse. *But I don't know what to say.* Then I thought, *He would probably reject my money.* I allowed this man to drive away, all the while feeling that I should give money to him.

When Joe came back to the car, I told him what had happened and how bad I felt that I let him leave. Joe said, "That is so weird. I felt God telling me the same, and I didn't know how to go about it."

I said, "Well, we will probably see him again."

By this time, we were driving down the road and Joe made a U-turn and said, "No, we are going to do what God wants us to do."

I said, "How can we find him?"

Joe said, "We are going to ride down this road and if it is meant to be, we will find him."

We drove about a mile and looked to the right, and he was pulled over at someone's home.

I managed to find $30 in my purse and gave it to Joe. He went up to him and another man said, "Can I help you?"

Joe said, "No, I need to speak to your friend." Joe told him, "Sir, I am a believer of God, and He asked me to give you this money and I don't know why, but you have a good day," and patted him on the shoulder. The man thanked him and looked ever so strange. I am sure he needed that money. We need to just do what God leads us to do and not ask questions.

I think I was embarrassed to only give him $30 but then I realized that $30 to him may be like $300 to someone else, especially if he is in need. I am sure he was or God would not have put it on our hearts to help him. We were very excited to find him and knew it was the right thing to do.

While Rhonda was deciding how to spend her leftover money, it was time to draw another name. Penny, the scheduling coordinator of Neighborhood Nurses, was the next name drawn. She had already given this thought and wanted to get food for Kris's friend and his four children. Penny stated, "I cannot stand the thought of anyone being hungry."

Penny ordered $93 of food from the Angel Food Ministries. This is a ministry where everyone can save on their grocery bill, while a dollar from each box of food that one buys goes to their community for families in need. I always thought that this was a ministry for poor people. It is a ministry for anyone, and poor people will be helped from the purchases that people make. Penny was killing two birds with one stone.

Penny purchased a Bountiful Blessing Box, Bread of Life Signature Box, and a Bit O' Blessing Box for this father and his four children. This was $93 of food that would last them a long time.

Like Rhonda, Penny also knew what hardship was. Her husband lost his job about the same time Rhonda's did and then was diagnosed with lymphoma. The past year had been tough for them as he went through chemotherapy. Thankfully, now he is in remission.

Penny is in her late fifties and has two beautiful daughters and four beautiful grandchildren. All of the people in our offices are very compassionate. That was a definite requirement to work for our company. When Joe and I started Neighborhood Nurses, we were aware that this was our ministry and God's business.

Joe and I also knew that in order to be successful in this business, we would have to raise the bar on healthcare, since this was a very competitive industry. I had to learn to give up a lot of the control and not to be a perfectionist. It took a lot of prayer to give this up. I remember the day the lights came on in my head. I realized that this is God's business, and it has nothing to do with my efforts, although God wanted us to put forth our best effort.

Rhonda came up with a wonderful idea for the remaining $23. She purchased transportation vouchers for patients to go to the doctor. She said that when her mom was alive, she was able to go to the doctor on vouchers that others had paid for. Again, another brilliant idea that I would never have thought of, because I didn't realize that someone could do that.

Penny decided that with her extra $7, she would purchase suckers and place Bible verses on them in order to go out and witness to people. This was another good idea that I would not have thought of. I was amazed at the bright ideas of our staff!

When the angel food came in the following Saturday, Penny met the friend's mom at the pickup site (which was a church), as the son was sick. The mom was very thankful, hugging Penny and telling her how much she appreciated the food. What a lot of food! Penny said there was more food this time than usual.

The next name drawn was our son, Kristofer. He manages our Wadesboro office. He is twenty-seven years old, born on October 31, 1983. We could not wait to see how he planned to spend the money. He started working with my husband at the age of ten. My husband owned his own business in minor construction and wallpapering. Kris saved his money and bought motorcycles, fixed them up, and sold them for much more money. Then he would buy more, fix them up, and sell them for even more.

Kris had always known how to make a dollar. He has three trucks in his driveway now that he purchased on his own at an early age. Two of them are older, but he is all for used items and fixing them up. He is also a handyman. He can fix anything.

chapter eight

Acts 20:35 I have shewed you all things, how that so labouring ye ought to support the weak, and to remember the words of the Lord Jesus, how he said, It is more blessed to give than to receive.

My hope is that other businesses will want to copy our project and go out and help in the community. It doesn't have to be $100 per person. It could be less or even more. I also hope that individuals will jump on the *giving* bandwagon. A lot of therapists suggest that depressed people should help others. There is no high better than that of helping someone. What a gift to oneself as well as the recipient. God always blesses the giver.

When I finished nursing school more than twenty-two years ago, someone in my community referred me to a family who needed a nurse to give their mom blood-thinning injections twice a day. I did this for a while and was asked to sit by this precious lady's bedside while she was dying. There is no higher honor than to share death with one of God's children.

During this time, I became close to the lady who took care of the patient every day. She cooked for her and cleaned her house. She was another very precious soul. When the patient died, this lady was without a job. For years, she had worked for this family, and all of a sudden, she was unemployed.

The children of the patient each gave her a day to come to their home, and there was one day left over. I had just become a nurse and had no idea if we could fit this into our budget, but I agreed to give her a day at our home. We had two small children and were on a tight budget. Somehow, we have been able to pay her for twenty-two years. Actually, we are the only ones who still have her cleaning our house.

She is so precious that my husband says when she gets too old to clean anymore, we will just pay her to come. She has such a sweet spirit. Our children also love her. We wanted to help her, and God worked it out so that we could. We reaped wonderful benefits from it. We are much better for knowing her,

My daughter-in-law and I do photography as a hobby, and it is a way of making extra money for personal spending. My sister-in-law's nephew asked us to photograph his wedding. I remember my own wedding. The fee just to photograph the wedding was outrageous. We could only afford about ten of our pictures. I knew this nephew wasn't rich, and neither was his fiancée.

I asked Jenifer what she thought about us just giving the photography of their wedding to them as a gift. She was all for it, because she has a giving spirit. We took more than two hundred pictures and gave them to this couple on a CD so they could print the pictures as they could afford to. How I wish I'd had someone do this for me! I remember my photographer telling me that he threw away the pictures that we did not buy. It just made me sick.

Joe and I each spent our $100 a few times over. We were just thankful to God that He had blessed us to do this. Each time we were able to help someone, we experienced so much joy! It seemed like God had opened the windows and poured out blessings to us, since we seemed to always have extra to give.

Kris finally decided what he would do with the money given to him. He was very excited that Joe and I had purchased Christmas for his friend's four children, but he knew his friend had sold his guitar earlier to help make ends meet for his family. Kris knew that his friend loved to play the guitar. Kris also felt that playing would be a stress reliever for him, since he was tied down with four children. Kris got on the Internet, and after a few days and a few negotiations, he had found a really nice guitar with the $100 that he had to spend. He was very happy. His plan was to give this to his friend at Christmas, because he knew his friend would not expect anything when we gave him the children's gifts.

The next day, Kris received a call from his friend. He said his friend told him that he was very embarrassed to have to ask him, but he needed money to purchase diapers for his baby. Kris said his friend sounded as though he had been crying. It broke his heart. Kris and Jenifer went to Walmart and purchased diapers and then gave the friend the rest of the $100 for gasoline, so he could take his children to and from school. I was really proud of Kris for helping his friend. Kris also said that if his funds allowed, he would purchase the guitar at a later date.

The next name drawn was one of our nurse supervisors, Zondra. She has always been compassionate and a strong Christian. Many times, I would ask her to pray with me for someone, and she would stop everything she was doing to pray. Zondra was married, with two beautiful little girls who looked just like her. Zondra was also turning forty the following month.

When I gave the $100 check to Zondra, she said, "I have to put it on my desk until I decide what I am supposed to do with it." I knew she would pray about it and take this project seriously, because she always took pride in her job and compassion in taking care of our patients. I also knew that it might even take her longer than one week to decide, so we went on and drew the next name, which was another one of our nursing supervisors, Karis.

Karis was also a registered nurse and was the same age as our daughter, thirty-one. Karis had two of the handsomest little boys. They were well behaved and just fun to be around.

She told me about how she was going to spend the $100 given to her. Her plan was to go to consignment shops and purchase gently used coats and hats for children at the homeless shelter. What an awesome idea! I was very proud of our employees and their thinking outside of the box. Another good reason for teamwork!

Penny was still excited about the project and asked if we could do it again after everyone completed their spending of the $100. I told her we would definitely keep giving, whether it is cash, time, etc. God expects all of us to give, since everyone can. Penny then told me how her life had been changed for the better since our revival. I was so happy to hear that.

After thinking about it, I realized that my life had also been changed. The business that we are in is very competitive. Some people were really put out when we started our agency, especially when we said we were going to raise the bar on healthcare. Because of some of the undermining actions of competitors, I had difficulty trusting a lot of people.

The evangelist in the revival made reference several times to how God wants us to be transparent. Initially, I thought, *Oh, no, that would be a sign of weakness* "feeling we did not need to expose ourselves to other agencies to do as they pleased as they knew our personal business. Then I realized that God said, "I will bless those who bless you and curse those who curse you."

chapter nine

1 Pet. 4:9 Use hospitality one to another without grudging.

Joe and I decided to have Thanksgiving at our home this year, since my mom had moved beside us. My dad died in 2003 and Joe's mom in 2009. My only living brother and his wife were remodeling their home, and it just seemed right for us to do so. This was the first time since our marriage that we had a holiday dinner at our home.

I planned and re-planned this meal; I wanted everything to be right. Joe's dad, sister, and her boyfriend would come, along with my brother and his wife, Mom, our son Kris, Jenifer, and their daughter, Peyton, and my aunt Lynn and uncle Jeff who had shared Thanksgiving with us since my mom was diagnosed with breast cancer in 1995.

Before the clock alarm went off, I awoke and sprang up from the bed at 5:20. I put the turkey in the oven and had other foods lined up to bake afterward. Jenifer, Mom, and Trish (my brother's wife) shared the cooking with me. The meal and the time with our family were perfect. We were very thankful for everything that God had given us.

When a person loses a loved one to death, the holidays can be pretty depressing. The first year of my brother and my dad's death was the most difficult. You have to experience their birthday for the first time without them, Father's Day, and all of the other holidays. We changed everything when we lost them.

We broke all of the traditions, and believe it or not, it was easier to tolerate. I remember having spaghetti the first Christmas after my brother died. It was almost humorous, because we had never had spaghetti for Christmas. You do what you have to do to mend your broken heart. I always wondered how non-Christians handled grief. I need Christ to wrap His arms around me when my heart is hurting. I also need the assurance that I will see my loved ones again.

While Zondra was still praying about the money she had to bless someone, Karis went to her boy's school and asked them to give her the name of a family that needed help. She also planned to buy the coats and give them away to children at a homeless shelter. Karis also needed more than one week to put her plan into play.

We went on and drew the next name, Tommy. He is a breath-alcohol technician for our drug screen company. He is also my brother. He is one year and eleven days younger than me. Tommy was one of my very best friends growing up, and we are still very close.

Tommy is married to a special person who he attended church with as a child. She is his soul mate. He was one of those who thought outside of the box. Tommy had friends on both ends of the spectrum. He has always been kind-hearted and always gave people the second chance that so many of them needed. When Tommy's name was drawn, it was three weeks until Christmas. We were excited to see what those three, Zondra, Karis, and Tommy, would do with the money. There were so many needs, because the economy had not changed much.

Karis found out that it was too late for the coats, since they had already distributed coats to the children.

She then decided to call the school where her young son attended and requested names of disadvantaged students. The guidance counselor gave her personal information on a boy and a girl without giving the names of the children. She was given sizes and wants for Christmas.

The items she purchased for the two children were really nice. She bought each of them a really nice outfit, underwear, socks, and hat. Then she purchased the toys that they requested. I was excited that this would be a very special Christmas for them.

Tommy also had a change of heart about how he would use the money that he was given. He and I had a dear friend who was struggling at the time, and he gave his money to pay this friend's power bill. I was very proud of him for doing that!

The giving continued in the office. All of our office staff was in "giving mode." We tried to meet all of the needs that we heard about. Many of them are not even mentioned in this book, but I guarantee you the Lord blessed us every time we blessed others. What a wonderful feeling.

This Christmas season was the least stressful that I have ever experienced. Along with the giving was a release of burdens. We need to just look around, and it will not take long to realize that we are blessed. We are doubly blessed when we have enough to help others, and we should thank our Lord for the blessings.

chapter ten

2 Cor. 9:6–15 But this *I say,* He which soweth sparingly shall reap also sparingly; and he which soweth bountifully shall reap also bountifully. Every man according as he purposeth in his heart, *so let him give;* not grudgingly, or of necessity: for God loveth a cheerful giver. And God *is* able to make all grace abound toward you; that ye, always having all sufficiency in all *things,* may abound to every good work: (As it is written, He hath dispersed abroad; he hath given to the poor: his righteousness remaineth for ever. Now he that ministereth seed to the sower both minister bread for *your* food, and multiply your seed sown, and increase the fruits of your righteousness;) Being enriched in every thing to all bountifulness, which causeth through us thanksgiving to God. For the administration of this service not only supplieth the want of the saints, but is abundant also by many thanksgivings unto God; Whiles by the experiment of this ministration they glorify God for your professed subjection unto the gospel of Christ, and for *your* liberal distribution unto them, and unto all *men;* And by their prayer for you, which long after you for the exceeding grace of God in you. Thanks *be* unto God for his unspeakable gift.

Zondra was still praying about the money she had to spend. We respected that, because she wanted to spend it the way God would have her spend it.

The next name drawn was Madge. She works three days a week, five hours per day. She is my mom, seventy-two years old. My brother and I had the honor of working with our mom and enjoyed it very much.

Joe and I hired her to do general office work. She had always been a hard worker, and it wasn't long before she was sweeping floors, mopping, cleaning our break room, and anything else she could do. I continually reminded her that we did not hire her for hard labor and that she needed to take it easy. Besides, we were all adults and capable of cleaning up after ourselves.

I remember as a child when mom came home from work. She came in full force, cleaning the house and cooking. She never relaxed, because there was always something to do with three children. No one has ever seen her home unclean. The last thing that she does at night is pick up and put everything in its place. She has always been a precious mother! She is very beautiful and young-looking too. My brothers and I liked for her to pick us up from school, since all of the kids would brag about how pretty she was.

My mom also made me very proud. My dad, her soul mate, died seven years ago, and as difficult as it was for her, she pulled everything together for my brother and me. She has been through so much in her life and still maintains a positive attitude. She is very compassionate and always putting others' needs before her own.

Mom was pregnant with our sister in 1961 when her appendix ruptured and she almost died. Our sister was born early and only lived six hours. Mom had survived two really bad automobile accidents as well as breast cancer. When my brother died, it must have been really difficult to pick up the pieces, but she did and went on for my younger brother, our children, and me. She was one of a dozen children born to her parents who lived in Chesterfield, South Carolina. She was never a stranger to hard times.

My mom did not go to work until my two brothers and I started school. I remember her reading Bible stories to us, and I also remember each week when she got paid, she would buy each of us a book. We were very excited to see what she chose for us. We always felt special, since she would pick a book that she thought fit each of our personalities. We loved it when she read to us.

Her grandchildren knew that she was very special and loved her like my brothers and I loved her. They loved to stay with her and often cried to stay overnight. Her great-grandchildren were also very fond of her and enjoyed staying with her. I had never seen a child who did not like my mom or one she could not win over in a couple of seconds. What a terrific woman!

Meanwhile, we gave Zondra a fortieth birthday party at the office. Her birthday was December 8. Karis had a black "over the hill" cake made, black balloons, and I made signs to hang announcing her age. Zondra told me that she still had not spent the money, because she was continuing to pray for direction.

Madge had called around and spoken with people about the homeless shelter and the needs of the people there. She first wanted to feed them; however, after talking to several people, she decided that there were some who attended Bible study at the homeless shelter who were not able to pay their power bills. This sparked my mom's interest, since the temperature had been in the teens. She also wanted to take some of the money and purchase a special gift for the lady who cleans our house, because she knew that she never bought for herself. This lady always looked after everyone else and was very sacrificing.

My mom looked forward to Tuesdays when this special lady came to our home. She loved to talk to her. They had become friends. They had a lot in common.

By this time, there was only one more name to be drawn, and it was another of our nursing supervisors, Valerie. She and I went back quite a few years. I had worked with her at a facility that housed mentally and physically handicapped children. She was such a good nurse and later worked private duty in the homes of some of our pediatric patients before becoming a supervisor for our Wadesboro office.

Valerie was very compassionate, often spending her own money to buy things that patients needed. Actually, that is a trait that each one of our nursing supervisors has. They are the very best. I would choose either one to take care of my very own loved ones. I had experienced firsthand each one going the second mile for our patients and for our company. How blessed we were to have them as our employees!

We received a thank-you card from my husband's sister's boyfriend, Nick. He thanked us for inviting him to Thanksgiving and told us that this was his first Thanksgiving after the death of his dad, and it was a good one. He said he could feel love in our home. We were very touched. We know that God owns everything. We do not live in a mansion; however, we just recently built one for my mom. Joe and I have always loved to invite people to our home and prepare meals.

We want people to feel welcome in our home. We also want them to see Christ in us. Giving is many things. It doesn't have to include money all of the time. Many people need to receive love. All of us can give love. What a blessing to soothe a hurting heart. We also enjoyed Zoey (Joe's sister) and Nick as much as they enjoyed being here. We have great love for them and all of our family members. We know God has blessed us with them.

Joe, his dad and sister are hurting from the loss of their mom. She died in May 2009. She was the glue that held this family together. We feel blessed that we got to spend time with her before she died, but there will always be an empty spot in our hearts for having lost her. Knowing she is living with Jesus makes it easier. With the loss of my brother, dad, and mother-in-law, the dynamics of both families have greatly changed. I am also proud of Joe's dad and sister, who have kept our family together, regardless of the pain.

chapter eleven

1 John 3:17–18 But whoso hath this world's good, and seeth his brother have need, and shutteth up his bowels *of compassion* from him, how dwelleth the love of God in him? My little children, let us not love in word, neither in tongue; but in deed and in truth.

The blessings from the giving project just poured in. That is not why we chose to do the project, but the Bible plainly says that you cannot outgive the Lord.

Joe and I received a refund from our health insurance policy of $2,855. We received a refund from our homeowners insurance of $385. Some of the assessments that I do outside of my regular job picked up, and I received extra funds for doing them outside of my county. Those are just a few of the many blessings that we have received.

Meanwhile, our nursing supervisor, Valerie, decided that she would give her money to one of our clients who did not have much. When we first admitted this client to our services, Valerie noticed that this person was missing a lot of essential items for everyday life and spent her own money to purchase things for the client. Valerie did not share this with me, but my son did.

Of all of our clients, this was definitely one who needed help, and we appreciated that Valerie chose to help this client. Valerie has always been a very compassionate person and has given her personal funds many times to help others.

Zondra finally knew what God wanted her to do with the money that she had. Another of our clients had children who would not be getting much for Christmas without help. As soon as Zondra heard of this, she went out and spent the money to help them. How exciting to know that she took a lot of stress off of this family while making some children's Christmas more joyful!

It is my hope that our twelve weeks of giving will encourage you to be a giver. Perhaps you have never practiced giving and you are not sure where to start. Pray about it, so that God will lead you. I have not told you every act of giving that we have done during this time, because I do not want to embarrass anyone. God led us to help several of those we employ, as well as family and friends. This book was never written to brag. It is to encourage giving and show you the importance of it in our everyday Christian life.

Our giving does not stop here, just as people's needs do not stop here. God expects us to give, and in doing so, He will always give His blessings.

Notes

Notes

Notes

Notes

Notes

Notes

Notes

Notes

Notes

CPSIA information can be obtained at www.ICGtesting.com
Printed in the USA
BVOW011822201111

276484BV00001B/60/P

9 781449 730192